And the Children Watched
A Reflection on the COVID-19 Pandemic

Written by Maureen O'Brien
Illustrated by Maia Kamenova

Copyright © 2020 by Maureen O'Brien

All rights reserved.
No part of this publication may be reproduced, or stored in a retrieval system, or transmitted in any form or by any means, electronic, mechanical, photocopying, recording, or otherwise, without written permission of the publisher. For information regarding permission write to Global Wisdom and Leadership Forum, LLC. Attention: Permissions Department, 1921 W. Wilson St., Ste. A, Batavia, IL 60510

And the Children Watched/written by Maureen O'Brien, 1st ed.
Based on the COVID-19 Pandemic
ISBN: 978-1-7349590-0-0

This book is dedicated to my grandchildren
Amy, Colin, and John,
and to all of the Heroes and Sheroes that gave of themselves
so lovingly during COVID-19, 2020.
Special thank you to Matt James for shepherding this book
to the world.

"Never doubt that a small group of thoughtful, committed
citizens can change the world. Indeed, it's the only thing
that ever has."
Margaret Mead

Once upon a time
in the year of the great pause
the world became sick
and its people became sick

...and the children watched.

And in the sickness
    heroes and sheroes began to emerge

They were brave beyond comparison because all they wanted to do was to help and to heal the world

...and the children watched.

The children saw their teachers on screens
  And they missed them desperately

The elders could not see their families
Or celebrate birthdays
Or hug

...and the children watched.

Powerful people showed up on every screen
  They pointed fingers at each other.

And they tweeted.

Yet people were still dying.
People were afraid.
Many people prayed.

...and the children watched.

Leaders told employees to work from home
    And moms and dads and aunts and uncles
        And sisters and brothers ...and dogs
            (and maybe cats)

Now had more time with each other in the same house.

The thing they had once longed for
Was now their gift

...and the children watched.

Then the restless started chanting.
 They shook their fists

  They proclaimed,
 "They had a right and they had a choice."

They would not stay inside.

And the heroes and sheroes began to weep
Was their good work forsaken?

...and the children watched.

No one denied that these were difficult times
different times, unprecedented times...
The heroes and sheroes continued to work
To hold up the world, and to help heal the sick

...and the children watched.

The children, once grown, told their own children
the stories of their experience
of the year of the great pause.
And when they did
they wept

They remembered the heroes and sheroes
who were willing to help the sick,
and to heal the world.
And all of this happened

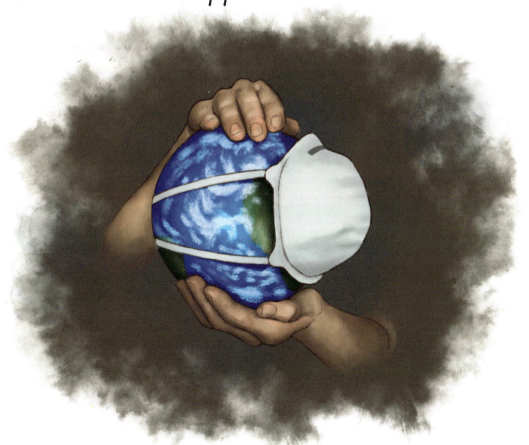

...while the children watched.

These were and are challenging times. What will the stories be of you as the children watch? Will they see that you did everything YOU could do to help and to heal? Will they say you were angry? Afraid? Pointing Fingers?

History and the children will recall the people that we have been in these times. Who will the children say you have been… as they watch?

All of the proceeds for this book (beyond expense of production) will be donated to FIRST RESPONDERS CHILDREN'S FOUNDATION (www.1strcf.org) on behalf of the Heroes, Sheroes, and CHILDREN of the COVID-19 Pandemic. Please support this worthy organization in any way that you are able.

There are simply not adequate words to express the depth gratitude of our hearts to the first responders, our Heroes and Sheroes. YOU have shown us what real leadership, (s)hero-ship looks like. Thank you for carrying us when we were not able to carry ourselves. We are forever grateful.

Sending so much love and light,

Maureen O'Brien

About the Author:
Maureen O'Brien, CEO, MOF

Maureen O'Brien is CEO of the Global Wisdom and Leadership Forum and is President of O'Brien & Son, Inc. The work of which O'Brien is most proud, (as identified in her signature line MOF -Mother of Four), is watching her children, Liam, CJ, Sean, and Lizzy, emerge into incredible adults who are and will continue to contribute much good in the world. She and her husband Dan have been married for 37 years and live in Illinois with their beloved dog, Riley.

In 2016, O'Brien faced her biggest challenge to date. She battled Stage IV Lymphoma... and won.

Contact O'Brien at www.globalwlf.com

About the Illustrator:
Maia Kamenova

Maia Kamenova is a student at Carnegie Mellon University, pursuing a B.A. in Architecture. Born in Bulgaria, she and her family immigrated to the U.S. early in her childhood. Maia has had a passion for drawing and painting her entire life, and now freelances as an illustrator. Her work spans a variety of subjects, like landscapes of the places she's traveled, architectural renderings, and portraiture. The media she most loves to work with are watercolor paint and drawing digitally. For this book she combined elements of both.

See more of Maia's work at her website, www.maiakamenova.myportfolio.com

CPSIA information can be obtained at www.ICGtesting.com
Printed in the USA
LVIW011158210520
656176LV00037B/1922